Dazzling Wobble

Judyth Hill

FUTURECYCLE PRESS

Mineral Bluff, Georgia

Published by FutureCycle Press
Mineral Bluff, Georgia, USA

ISBN 978-1-938853-18-0

Contents

Dedication

for, of course, JRM

amanwhoputstape&chalk/stringonsidewalks&pretendstotakemeasurements
buthopesodd
shadowsmightbeinstructive.

Among his other gifts...

&

my *sine qua non...*

Rockmirth

Qui dono lepidum nouum libellum
Arido modo pumice expolitum?

∞

...quare habe tibi quidqudi hoc libelli
qualecumque; quod, o patrona uirgo,
plus uno maneat perenne saeclo.

Who shall receive my new-born book,
My poems, elegant and shy,
Neatly dressed and polished?

∞

...take this little book
for what it is, my friend.
Patroness and Muse,
Keep these poems green for
A day or so beyond a hundred years,
O Virgin!

—Gaius Valerius Catullus,
translated by Horace Gregory

8

Wake up heart!

Wake up!
You've slept too long in the iron bed of yearning.
You've slept too long.
The bedclothes are slovenly.

Get up & make that bed of a heart!
The alarm has gone off.
What time is it?
It is now! And you are late!

Ha! I can't be late for now, you say...
That's right!

Silk Camisole

Love on a hot day—
bouquet of weak in the knees
dark night toss and turn
twisted sheets

wind in the pines,
the way sand stays warm
long after dusk, and still
the waves of that sultry sea wash in and in.

O
it's part tropical,
mostly mountain,
rimrock above timberline
a long way to down
where ferns grow in dense underbrush,

Hell, it's Russian Olives come to bloom in May,
crazy moon rise any month,
you know that aroma surely.

It's a woman on lovefire,
all ember and gleam,
whiff of dark chocolate
waft of jasmine ginger,

rampant sweetness
on a breeze of cove and cave,
the hidden, the mysterious,
the arcane, other languages,
lost keys, amethysts
and labyrinth.

Come find me, this scent says,
I am a doorway woman,
watching rain fall
in the green canyon.

"There's No Place the White Clouds Can't Go"

—Shu Shan K'uang Jen
9th Century Chinese

Nowhere the plumage of doves and angels
isn't moving
over the dusty stairways of the Ancient City.

The Moorish tiles spell

as always, the name of God
in letters of fire,
in the shade of blue that is exactly your eyes after love.

I know both those loves.
They take wing inside me,
as if I were an invented city
and you had designed the streets.

I am all plaza and gazebo, 100% zocalo
where women
in long silks spin in an ecstasy of Godfire.

That is how it is entirely.

Just like that.

Ajah, Ajah,—
Come to me as if you are me
and I will come to you.

Every alley, every sidewalk
crack is breathing in enormous broken joy.

You know we have come at last home
because we can't see anything here
that is not already the Beloved.

Dazzling Wobble

Ask a question and the place will answer.
Does it matter what you ask?
Desire is a mad alcoholic on a binge of furious.
Wander that jungle and even the star fruit will catch fire.
You will be cooked, then digested by the wind.
It will feel like an answer coming from the West, or maybe the North.
Dreams or prophecy? You'll have to ask.

You'll pack a bag.
Egg sandwiches in waxed paper, packets of pens, and the beliefs
of monastic nuns tattooed on your palms.

If Death moves his foot to the left, what is your next move?

You will need oxygen to know, but have somehow grown gills,
so must sip water for the intelligence of fish.

Butterflies and ocelots lend a certain credence as well.

The map is a discontinuous pattern; connect the dots, but quickly.
Memorize the fleet departure of anything but yourself.
You have slowed to clocktime,
tick tick tick....

This is the cadence of handiwork, crochet or cross-stitch.
At least there will be fabric; the warp and weft
might imply your destiny.

Somewhere there is definitely a library,
across water one would think.
Have you been? Can you imagine this?

Sipping tea, you might conjure the shelves,
then the book, carelessly replaced, that extends just a bit.

It is in that one: the script, cursive, italic,
the first letter illuminated, foxes and lions rampant in the borders,
a hint of the ferocious, but doable.

Maybe you are familiar with a word or two.
You quickly recognize the letter from certain ways
that women, their arms bangled with silver, dance in rain, of chimes.

You are sure, or almost sure, you are onto something
when you hear the tang of E natural,
inhale the scent of blood oranges,
remember that the ticket to Granada
(wrapped around the ocelot's tooth)
is still tucked in your back pocket.

It's the money they spend in dreams.

You will meet Garcia on the stairs overlooking the *Plaza Civiles,*
or was it the balcony of your rented room,
on the 5th day of August, 2 weeks before his death?

He has a poem for only you.

You always knew this, but could only arrive by forgetting

everything except his dark eyes, his request for a coffee
that afternoon,
just before *las cinco* and the chorus of rifles.

Does your arriving change anything?
We have to believe that it could.

Keys and palm trees and jaguars and dolls
with porcelain faces
have to have the golden bones of antiquity somehow inside them.

This is the only way to be strong.

The sheer audacity of getting out, closing the door behind you,
learning the language, even badly,
is the answer and you know it.

100 Views of the Floating World

Grant me the spiral staircase of kiss,
the real skin-to-skin ascent.
Grant me the bluebird of such crazy happiness,
feathers to match the horizon of outrageous loving;
I promise famous embraces and incendiary politics.

I long
to be the dusting of snow on the Mt. Fuji of you,
your cherry-lipped geisha *avec* jasmine tea and cloud cover,
a strummed shamisen, pure futon.

You are the manners brought to my grandmother's table,
salt cellars, cloth napkins,
set silver, and please.

I, a horseshoe of desire, your bauble of lucky,
I'll ring and ring, make you such music
as does measure what tilts us on the scale of golden,
turns you iron.

Milky Way thrown 'cross the bed sky of night,
Orion *in flagrante,* o my *delicto,*
October is a wind we cannot ride,
a blur; take the leaves, then take them,
I have others fashioned in your honor.
You are magnetic north; I'll spin there.

A miracle: Fahrenheit of pleasure, you and me,
what is utterly spoken sinuous, both shedding and enrapt.
Written language aside, everything spells original temperature.
All commas point home.
Where was I ever going,
but to you?

Lay me down, then, in the lap of the divine, candles kindled,
wine poured and new bread:
whole loaves, baked for the constancy of snow geese.

You are apple trees in full flush, doors of the temple open,
the polish of marble.
It's the rub of love—tectonics of dream—
how, ardent, we can constellate into ancient shine.

I sign my name on your lips
for practice, I sew on your buttons,
make cream soups daily, simmer and stir.

I am a student of indoors and learning quickly.
I know your place, almost.

Sweetheart, this poem needs you! Come quick!

This page is incessantly made white by your absence:
you are this ink, this flowing away and towards,
these joyous words, these.

Outside in America

She feels strongly about blue.
Cobalt always, especially blown glass.
Sky blue only as in Storrie Lake sometimes, Wyoming, her mother's eyes,
Matisse's wallpaper.

As she falls asleep, she imagines beds of sweet clover.
Rolls onto her right side, knees to chest, rinses her brain
of any thought but field.

She went first ever to Corsica.
Has mica, a chunk, glittering, in her purse.
Was it from there? She hopes so.
She remembers nothing from that trip,
except the light that first morning.
Coffee in a porcelain cup, thin smoke of fragrant steam rising.

The room had high ceilings and she was alone.
Spoke to no one for days. Wrote letters, left-handed, that time.
She had packed a white dress, a jade scarf, a buttercup-yellow bikini.
Not a thing else,
except a photograph of the great Tor in Scotland, a box of mints,
a novel in French, which she didn't read, couldn't,
because she did not read French.

On the train through London she looks out the window
and plans sumptuous menus for 8-, 10- and 12-course meals
including amuse-bouche and tart sorbets to cleanse the palate.
She dreams in juggernaut gold, whatever that is,
has a cat that actually lives next door, only visits.

She closets 7 pairs of shoes.
Red Tony Lamas, white silk ballet slippers,
assorted Frederick's of Hollywood stilettos
that lace way up her legs. That's all,
that and barefoot and a secret pair of black fuzzies with Panda faces.

She has sworn how glad she is to be a painter so many times that she believes it.
It isn't true. Her palette this year is sea green, mint green, corn silk yellow,
Chinese red. She has recently learned to play the Gamelan, for herself only.

Subsets of neurons are surreptitiously linking in her mind.
She listens to Coltrane on vinyl, loves both Brontë sisters,
has seen Dersu Uzala countless times.
Fervently admires Love Song of J Alfred, the Potomac by moonlight,
turned maple, the Urals, and Gauguin's women.
They are a flavor to her, echoed on her spice shelf.
Cardamom, nutmeg, allspice; green, pink and white pepper.

Under her bed are her calendars for the last 16 years,
a hat box with something of her mother's—she nearly remembers what—
a bag of sea shells from some coast, a set of Nana's silver.

She wears Amorous lipstick, Obsession parfum,
black black eyeliner, a cheap drugstore brand.
Drinks champagne, cold and too much, and loves cream soups.
Her middle name is Madeleine; she sees in the dark,
reads the fine print of instructions in Italian.
Her music box would play *Au Clair de la Lune* if she would let it.
It is August, and she has a bruise on her left arm.
From what you don't want to know.
Her phone number is 301-247-8286, she would love to hear from you,
she'll never call.

The weather we make

Mirror, cracked saddle, scent of basil,
the chambray shirt you wore that night,

all, all for you, leaves
swirled—you knew they would—

you yourself, darling, my darling,
had warned me.

You said golden, you said, wait.

I didn't listen. Couldn't.
I said between us a flower, the petals, like the swords of Cordoba.

Pierce me, I said, I asked you,

because you are generous.
Because you are my love.

Slow down and meet the fast god

Slip between moons into solid fragrance.

Memorize the wisdom written on the face of glaciers.

Keep walking.
If this is the day the ground opens,
then it is.

Bake a cake of many grains, and go down.
You will lose your mother and gain a recipe.

Follow the rules:
Eat nothing,
don't linger.

Love the fierce beauty of the taken daughter that is yourself.

Track mountain lion into the den of the invisible;
become snake and vice
versa; curl & swirl, shimmer into *Vendredi,*
into Kali Durga, Pele, and *La Diosa de Las Serpientes,*
clamor of skulls around your waist.

Slip between seasons into the mythology of river.
Turn as aspens do, both under and gold.

Flicker into ripe.
Rhyme with sideways, with bangle, with breathless and the first
word for chaos you can think of—
the light right now is such a good guess.

Keep going.

Learn what is good enough to say twice.

Let's tangle with undying love—
take it on, take it on—

take on a round of immortal, burn all
the way to ash, and rise as berry.

Hunter's Moon: come find me.
I'm in full décolleté camo,
dressed as cattail and raven's caw, braceleted in fallen grasses.

If you are first frost, let me be your early thaw.

We'll make a supple weather out of amnesia, inscribe
remembering on clouds.

I want to dive, Janos, into your name,
nimble one, all clues aside;
I'll come up hooked.

Reel me in, back to this world,
from that;

I wriggle, good god, moon fish,
shining in your breathing hands.

Arsenic Beloved

That cello played them:
they were night's crescendo,
mountain as encore.

The moon's road glittered,
Cordoba, Cordoba—

100 roses and so the horses flew,
as she to him, both leaves and falling.

He swirled in a disdain of gold she applauded, wrapped
in his cape of daggers.

Whatever they had thought was distance
was caught in the temperature of lips, in the tangle of hands.

From full to dark and back is not so far,
in the compass of wind.

Little Vision of the Great Intangible

Some vowels disappear,
some arc across lines of poetry,

black etched ravens that have lately been cawing, cawing;
their wings are consonants, or would be.

In the hardness scale, there is no measure for my heart:
neither talc nor ruby.

Streak across me, as lightning in the canyon sky.
Leave marks; tattoo divine on my skin.
Ink me into rain.

Say my name, and I call you into flame,
my secret treasure, my astral tango.

I go to petals, fragrant, the finality of garden in October:
burnt umber, sienna, wild thistle and mourning dove.

It's the puzzle we solve by putting the box away.

I am porous. You are crazy weather, fallen apples, the chokecherries
gotten entirely by jays, mullein stalk gone to pillar and seed,
the fallen parts of the wisteria I sweep at my doorway each morning,
what wakes me to startle, redwing and cirrus.

You arrive in my afternoon, a pot of tea already brewing, hot on the hot
stovetop, coals in the grate, bread in the oven, past ferment, into seize
and risen.

Golden, sesamed, open that lid—you have the words—
the scent of welcome is over us, a Giotto nimbus, the smoke after the train
leaves Finlandia station, a revolution in the air.

None will be left behind this time; gather us all, all into peace, for once,
you can, you can.

Whatever happens to us
is in the capable hands of the maple's scarlet leaves.

Whatever you do next
is how the peach tree will remember us.

Let us go then, you and I

where iambics
billow, pillow, and I sigh.

This is how syllabic winds
might shift weather:

chance of, I say, and mean, us;
mean storm & riptide and the way stairs collide
with sudden arrival, so that

down and up are not directions, but collaborative fragrance
posited by ancient texts only recently
recovered.

Now we'll be, and buzz.

It's a sound theory, how fast to travel
on asphalt ribbons of negative entropy.

I skid towards the guardrail in waltztime,
as if my life had rehearsed Act 3 of Black Ice
and learned the lines at last.

Finally we are there & together.

Send home the children,
send them; I'll cook, you'll breath. We'll take turns
at happiness, divide the labors of love.

Slow to 2nd gear and safety.
Question the politics of invasion.

Your life depends on it and mine;
reading Eliot is still the cure for the disease we swear
we don't have.

So paint it, that blue behind clouds,
the interrupt rhythm of 200 cloistered rememberers.

I still believe in 770 mph of poetry,
still believe you touch me from 100 years and states
away.

You whisper couplet & dream, streetlight & fog.

Hearing your voice,
I wake
from drowning
in professional America.

Olly Olly Oxen Free

Looked up over beautiful food,
Cambozola, red wine from the desert,
slices of newly made bread: velvet crumb,
crisp crust.

Said that name
a certain way, long consonant sound
at the end.

Then some other thing happened.
Then another. There is always traffic,
missed calls, voicemail, text messages
from elsewhere.

We listened, listened,
to the frequencies of absence
as if we might miss something.

All of us are hiding out in God.

If we stop searching right now,
we could be found.

Jacks or Better, Deuces Wild

If you cannot remain before my eyes
please give me back my heart.
—Qawwali love song

That day you left, surefire Epiphany, minus King's cake,
straight ahead Bourbon Street: fol de rol, rollick, a hoot and a holler.
Me, a stone's throw into snowbound, you.

Soon-to-be, crayfish and bayou, red beans, rice, then blues and jazz
serious, drinking all night, no distress, that's right, no rose, disrupt
or nightingale's song, women slung off balconies, ex-lovers

after the white-knuckled, pine-rimmed, yellow-line ice
obscured onslaught, but easy:
velocity as destiny.

Pretty simple: just turn the key and there's the road.
Not desire, just late-night dithyrambs, a hiss
on the radio through the Texas panhandle, petroleum reek—

it's a crap shoot always, isn't it just—
7 come 11, a dice roll, between the engine's well-pitched whine
and the body's sweet enigma;

10 damn fine lines written on both sides of a brown paper bag,
fame and fortune almost from breathtaking good will, stand up loud
and aloud; no money, but lots of whiskey, a few nightmares, braceleted arms,

embracing in the dark…of what: solar flares, lunar tilt, Iraq, Somali,
no-fault insurance; you're guaranteed solid iambic, 96% mystery, lucky you.
So close to what could possibly be construed as possible.

Drive away then, it's a measured bet there's a room somewhere in this state
or the next, or the one after that; that's what the West is for, really,
to stretch out and remind us of America.
Make the rear view mirror into a story that's memorable, scans good.

Don't look up too soon, kiss me quick, toothpaste and a thermos
of coffee steaming. Some kind of pie.
What does this remind you of, exactly what?

Back up and hurtle forward, and why not, I mean, come on,
there was no reflection in the glass, hence no grievance
you'll have to worry about.

Shoelaces are what the teacher
taught us, and I learned to trip and fall down. Good at it too, very.
Got up. Somewhere you are still driving, or maybe not.

There's *amor fati* here, a gate, negative capability, Tchaikovsky's Piano
Concerto, the first, Olson on projective verse, Townsend's Solitaire, snowfall
and safety, Gillespie at Carnegie with Ella and Charlie, how's that, and alone,

Wittgenstein in the early a.m., still sharp, lines from Creeley, let's hear it
for hardcore thinking, the very edge of festive dreaming, so much like
a holiday, a catered affair, the, man-oh-man, way gone thing.

And we go on burning,

fierce, gravitational pull: mass of the moon at escape velocity,
that impact, the wobble of it,
our wobble, making climate and magnetic tides.

We go on burning, and the ratatat of city traffic,
strum of setar, rain's tympani,
and the brain's random crap shoot
at some shine or brilliance astound.

You're alone or not.
It hardly matters anymore.

You drive all night; it's such a good excuse for home.
A valiant attempt, let's say.

Anyone who didn't know me, my penchant for drama & vodka on the rocks,
would say how well I know about bow'd neck and white feathers,
also beauty.

I can live with anything except what you left me with,
and that's not even discussable.

Sat in the bathtub for hours the last night.
Winter stars whirled on overhead, the Chariot, the Swan.
Told time by constellations and my skin's slow pucker.
Listened for the next thing, whatever it would be.

I'm not trying to get over this just yet.

Rose petals and red wine, one submersion at a time,
I decided.
I'm going to go on burning.

Beverages and Dissonance

The body's over
and there's less and less to say.
—Bob Dylan

That's where it goes, but if the phone rings, pick it up.
Say hello slowly.

It's a cold day.
In this town, the baseball diamond's empty,
and the scrub oaks in the grove alongside Sprenger's place arch bare.

Everything, if you can believe it, feels like the first time.

Frickin' emotions.
A lot like weather: blow in, blow out.

A fifth grader I teach says, "Liar, get the hell out of my face,"
in an Exorcist voice to a 4th grader who races away.
I love the crazy knot of being the adult.

Storms are predicted that don't come.

You never came back, and anyone could have predicted your absence
breathed into every line break the way
you cleared the table after breakfast,
stacked wood in a small-to-large sequence.

Watched magpies and house wrens from what I would have called my porch
before I knew I'd have to remember you there.

I dreamed in the night of bath salts and bad gin,
that you were coming back to return my watch.
One hand had wrung loose and time dangled awry.
Minutes clinging to some uphill excursion called fall and spring.

I wrote Urdu verses of such longing, or Farsi,
or an abstruse Punjabi dialect—how can you know?

I don't speak dream.

But it was nearly like sleep, wasn't it?

I want winter back. It's got to be January; we deserve one,
don't we?

Stomp and swear, get entitlement confused with beverages
and open-book tests, which I easily fail
because I will not turn the page.

Close the book, close the damn book you could tell me, if you were not
on the Interstate you took off on in the beginning of this poem.

You're just a cup of coffee away and that's everything.

Something Something Something Called Something

He imagines the lemon groves of Malaga
and the maritime night of Cadiz.

She destroys her heart in a January of sensation,
the cracked mercury of her mirror.

Crowned by the roses of constant lightning,
he is both storm and the icy skin of pond.

What disturbs is dazzle.
What connects is the treble spiral of the clarinet's windfall of sound.

In the world of music
they are rich, and together.

Play me, play me loud, she says.
Without your voice,

my night's empty as birthed egg.
Also as incipient.

The yoke of distance weighs lightly.
Visit me with your vivid echo—

I'll braid your absence into my hair,
wear you as charm, benevolent

attractor, lyric balance.
What snows our snows have seen,

lit by quiet, and that bough-bent falling
through bars of light.

Only the Holy

The bed is not made and the bread is not kneaded
and the bells that rang in the temple of the woman alone
did not summon the quiet one,
whose broom does not sweep the leaves,
the leaves that did not fall.

After the snow did not fall, because snow had already fallen
and the echo of those bells already rung out
into a room so filled with empty
you'd have to invent bowls and bones
and nests and baskets to write this:

you have to plant a peace rose.
Prune it over seven seasons & save the thorns
from the cuttings. Write love spells on white candles.
Light those candles in the empty rooms
that look out on snowy fields, scrub oaks bare of leaves.

Then, then, then
will the bells wild ring,
will the bread rise,
and we, two, we, beloved, will to our shared bed go,
to dream the garden that will grow that rose.

Measure for Measure

Gobray: to fall into a well unknowingly...
Onsra: to love for the last time...
—*archaic, lost South Asian dialect*

Moth wings sheathed in scales
translating wave to color in that particulate language of light.

It's refraction, not pigment, the artist told me, and I knew
I needed a river.

Need color by proxy, by vibration and distance, by the slant reveal
of deep time minus the sting of judgment.

I want the *roundthebend* mystery, the *Idon'tknow* next of it.
Like real life.

There is, in my future, as yours, beautiful work and stupid work.
There are children and poems.

Burn in desire. Stay up late, circling the flame.
Read books in bed, pillowed and alone, not lonely.

This is only possible by taking sometime flight,
lost: calling home miles and centuries later.

Hurtling Buoyant

Where were we when we first knew happiness?
It must have been a sunny day on the Avenue of Faith;
we were just leaving
and the new ones just arriving, anyway singing, such originality
such cadence and merit, they might have been psalms—
praise in the licking cat's tongue, a friction we call language.

I know another word or two in that language,
and each a source for weeping or, in some cultures, happiness.
My left brain recites the psalms
that serve as stop signs on the Avenue of Faith,
my right records tremendous originality:
cones and rods in discord, the strategy of leaving

unseen, what can only be seen by leaving.
This is the battle cry of language,
easily occasioned by raccoon scat, blackbirds and originality.
And, for once, I settled for that happiness
on the Avenue of Faith,
subject of sonnets and psalms.

Walking in the shadow of psalms,
arrivals feel strangely like leaving.
Since we made these deals on the Avenue of Faith,
coming and going are synonyms in the dark language
of happiness.
Which is how we court our originality,

by never seeking originality.
Singing instead *Canto Hondo,* fevered elegies, and psalms
to the tune of rain water and frog—such happiness,
as if all history is the lyrics to a fiction we call leaving,
because we haven't yet learned the grief-stricken language
spoken on the Avenue of Faith,

if in fact there is any speaking on the Avenue of Faith.
Maybe we seek originality
by designing nooses, shakers, dizzying vaults of language
instead of psalms
so we'll never be arriving or leaving.
And so cling to an easier happiness

than happiness as we could know it on the Avenue of Faith.
Where all leaving is a set of carefully creased maps to originality,
all psalms made of beebalm and kisses, in some sorrowing, creaturish language.

Slow Dancing Fast

Like hand and foot, ear & glove,
we are undone, splash of time,
que narcotic.

Washed in a clock of words, speedway of desire,
TransAm soda pop curlicue—

Frieze, the worthy Egyptian, papyrus—
paper veldt, jungle of a page where language tangled,
tangoed in the blue vein darkness of hair.

Stomach falling off cliffs only to wake in the orangutan night.

What a blitzkrieg of a summer, a hellhole,
land-mined with conversation, bric-a-brac, nuanced cocktails,
feathered windpipes.

You said what you thought.
Ghosts mopped the kitchen from a pail of stars.
Lead buckets trailed up stairs.

We felt rather than heard.

Clocks washed in words:
butter and rock rim.
I wouldn't trade it, trade it for anything
though I grew steadily shorter, peevish,
and finally made entirely of exotic wood.

The same mosquitoes flew on the ceiling as earlier.
Peacock blue, the effervescent fan of night
almost meant something.

I thought it did.
I wrote it could.

I appealed to a higher court of finesse,
to the lynchpin of kinky sex—
desk weights, I think you call them—
tower of feathers that fall inside a glass fist
pretending to be, no, wishing to be, no, lurking as if—
snow.

I was cryogenic anyway, pretty me.
Slaphappy into the 15th-century Jersey-ridden cosmos
where the sea combs out the shore for pleasure's sake,
a street walker, floozy
wet as this canyon between the legs of monsoons.

I had the baby here—I did—and the ruination
and the face peel, peculiar ruminations of tadpoles:
they were thoughts, the rescued ones,
that swam and poured down the throat of ponds.

I just couldn't lick it,
couldn't beat them,
couldn't join them,

couldn't think of one clever purpose to ring the paler clauses into vivid.

Stopped being clear, or shiny—
talked to grosbeaks, sent letters to dogwood,
had an affair with two syllables.

And why not? After 13 years
hadn't I married? Hadn't I chosen this disaster?
Hadn't I made my bed, now sleep in it,
if you can, if you dare.
If daybreak ever comes, I'll give you something to cry about.

You can stand and be counted on the fingers of one hand.

The left—like a what?
A Tantric nightmare?

What a puzzle for losers, for pencil pushers
and Five & Diamond hopes.

A lidless pocket that keeps leaping open,
saying, "Look at my empty, just look at it—
I told you this would happen, you so and between."

Don't curtail anything, not a bit of May June July August.

Clamor!

Wrath, anger, that Orion's belt strangles—
but it's a map anyway.
You could go there, I think you could.
Rage is a bitter stallion with a good sense of direction.

I smelled orange peels & glass breaking.
That's the last symptom, they say,
when you finally have nothing to say
and it pours out; they worm it out of you—
sidewalks, doorknobs, porch swings.

Doesn't matter:
there's nothing left to describe.

We had the garage sale after all the years of storage.
What did it matter what we kept or didn't?
At least the summer answered that.
It was a question of roses,
of what ate the buds before bloom.

We gave it a college try,
the full-blown educational riptide.
Though if you looked, you'd only have seen a vase,
water and a valiant streak of creased petal.

There were no ashes involved. There wasn't a fire.
That was last year's trick, and it was safer.

We babbled like a brook & put it out in words, talk, language.

We said soothe & turquoise & bright ruby bead.

Our prayers were whole, were made of leavened bread, of whistles,
cloth rosaries, of what mattered: our fathers, our mantras,
our glowworms, our triple caves, our three-way beacons.

That alarm sounded.
Sounded good.

I can't go to Roswell, or breakfast, or anywhere
even infinitesimally green.
I'm also itchy. That's part of it.
I'm unable to get ready get set
or tell a joke.
Popular—see, that's my best go.

I gave it a whirl and it went:
down a pile of months that rattled and clanked
like the chains they really were.

I didn't wake up from this dream;
I wrote it, flayed and torn open.
A carton the Fed-Ex men brought to ground,
it fit between lilacs and the Datura going to ferocious seed.

Even the flowers had teeth, and the moon wasn't the moon
but a criminal that escaped the clutches of valuable.

I'm too young for this.
Also too old.
I've worn out the welcome of all my past poems.
But so what?

What I have to say can wear any old thing.
Isn't that what the flea market's for?
To get a deal on what someone else doesn't want and you do?

Place settings, dust bowls, odd weather, Kansas even.
Whole states no one has any more use for.
In Utah, entire family trees go up for grabs.
So pathetic, it's taken 800 pages to finally go liquid.

We must have had practice to have worked this dissolve so well,

so angular—not a pitfall did we miss.
Anvils, closets, whole shelves of books—good ones—
moved from room to room, relabeled mine, then yours.
But it never got dangerous, stayed socks and undies.

Simple transfer of custody,
no jury, no court, no episiotomies.
Everything just ran out.

You could say it looked like normal gravity—
what you'd get if you turned the bucket,
the whole kit and kaboodle, upside down.

But why would you, why would you?

That's the question from forsythia to asters.
Why the rose?
Why the sackcloth?
Why reschedule the *Dia de los Muertos*?

Why make more holidays of grief;
why throw peaches into reverse?
Why make summer into velvet, or water, or dark gold
or epoxy, or windows, or a jangle of monks
weaving up the mountain, ringing bells and begging for rice
or weeping—take your choice.
I certainly did, and what a time I had,
I had,

From grape hyacinth to chrysanthemum.

Enjambment by Sextant

I was as I was, leonine, I guess, amber-clad,
dressed in a blaze of departures, four-fold equinoctial woman,
packing only ice skates and pencils,
secret diagrams of ladders for breathtaking escapes
plotted in blue shells, my opal calcinated skin, the sheen and shine of gone.
I masqueraded as mirror, shed light on myself,
rhymed with inner mercury—O I was a lake of sometime fire!
And dappled in green, the underneath kind, the verdant underpinning of forest.

Come alive, you wind you! Be feast or at least
garden, come coreopsis and spider mum, and ah lullaby breeze.
Temper, temper, stormwhirl—see how the letter A glitters in all 8 volumes
of our encyclopedia—how the jaguar's beaded skull
inhales the authority of this room. Whistler painted it, they say,
in buttercup yellow, scent of sweet beeswax, tulip poplars, their
three-leaved miscellaneous splendor. Or was that the train station
in Orléans? Stained glass, the Maid herself in flames,

and the bells bells bells in cathedral towers chiming, everyone suddenly
an ambassador of beauty, succinct indigo, all the swish and
verve of stanza and desire. Virtue, at last, is its own amethyst bird.
I've said that before, somewhere before, all the clocks struck fierce and
skittered the season's alarm: Gambel oak in full leaf—huzzah!
This canyon, a box of events, of crayons newly minted, all colors unknown,
tight in a sweet fist of the little one, not afraid to get it right!
We invent, at last, a quicksilver fabric, Wednesday's alphabet.

Akin to Japanese—deliciously vertical, a wasabi sneeze!
Finally there is no crisis, just perfectly acclimated sedition,
and the good people, the real heroes: echinacea, blue columbine.
Once upon a time, she had a table, an argument, a hatbox, a nest of starlings.
This time she has enormous weather, a liter of mountain, 6 geese a'laying,
five gold rings. Not to mention the horned owl, chamisa in bloom.
This is the lair of woe & light! *Quelle surprise!*
The bright scales balancing. The up and someways down of really growing.

It's onomatopoeic, isn't it? Tie everything you own to a stick
and set it on fire. Get going pronto. A way to be iron arrives.
Consider singing in the ancient voice of the bellows.
The time for snow blind and microbe is over. The force field
could win by sheer evaporation and standards of mercy. Nothing hurts
for once, nothing. Except is missing the other 2 lines, amputees:
another graceful landscape of little anarchies. Not for sale to me,
or you, but available on a trial basis. Sign here, on the ropes, in the slant line
of silence that was always the countdown to this time all done.

Answer this with

Do not accept the heart
that is the slave of reason
—Qawwali lyric

spent mullein stalk, staven hut at forest's edge.
This is how we'll live: in utterance, in spoken embrace
of rapturous apart and sudden grace. No maps,

but the ridgeline swirled in fog, a sweeping
sound the ground makes under snow.

Language is fence, is exchange of valuables
on the heart's black market.

Indigo is your breathless catch of kiss, flavor of fevered cinnamon,
cumin and later.
Spilt silence, no use crying.

Snow falls through the interstice of minutes
in an hourglass of January storm.

I'm waiting, I think I am.

Smoke curls over chickadee lyric,
the birth cry of cottonseed:
Auriga and Corvus whirl overhead.

You decide to sing
after a recurring dream of your voice soaring skyward
in the shrine of Hazrat Chishtie, at Ajmer,
where you have never sung, not you nor your father, nor his.

But you will, surely you will.

Bring me closer to God, I beg you, or hold me all night in your arms.
Bed me down in fervent desire, under black Lilith moon,
Hecate moon, moon of the triple veiled ones, Manat, Al-Lat, Al-Uzza.

Roll me over, you know exactly how,
or palm to palm, wouldn't it have been, or close:
I love always, you, despite, or because of, the unreasoned heart.

Coals embered in the hearth,
tie my story to a spindle and you'll get a skein of gold.
Up one sleeve is piney woods,
the other secret's the Volga's icy run;
it's an old, old tale where we dance and marry in the original Russian.

My dowry is the darkness in Rembrandt,
slant of shine in Vermeer.
A set of colored pencils, what Alyosha told Ivan at the end,
hiss of samovar.
Millet bread and Kandinsky's madness.
I'm rich and desirable, yes?

500 light years ago, fires roar in Orion's left knee,
but we see them now, tonight.
Here the white kitten yawns prettily. Such science

as we still possess says find your lover in the North,
trace winter light in spruce shadow on swales of fallen snow,
embanked cold, the spun startle of black birds.
Be prepared for anything, absolutely anything.

God is Wind in the Horse's Mane

The corners of my mouth.

An unmade bed.

In Seville, walking somewhere,
you whistled & I thought, I make him happy.

Amanitas and the Pleiades tag-teamed.

What I understood was silence and your voice.

Fields of Icelandic poppies
burst into maniac avenues of cored wealth:
such gold as I have is yours in true poem.

In the blue heron part of this story, you are alive,
peeling an orange for breakfast, reading poems
on the balcony of the rented apartment off the *Séptimo Barranca*.

Another woman wrote the part with the oranges, but I don't think she'll mind.

There was always enough time, just.

I have a coffee; you, tea.

Section by section, I watch you piercing thin skin into tart juice.
Something is waking all the way up: bells in a sunlit city,
snow blossoms, a silver spoon stirring,
famous loving, sheets Egyptian cotton, tangle and tenor of text and texture.

Silk to velvet, I see your mouth on mine and raise you
Kiri Te Kanawa's *Aïda,* Harold Lloyd hanging from any building,
Frost's journals, masking tape on asphalt, talking all night in the Trieste,
young gorgeous men & their saxophones, good coffee in the right cup.

It's very complicated, my teacher would have said,
because of what she knew about everything.

She measured love against global eco-cultural-cross-time
mythopoeic/seasonally specific/glaciers/ mountains—
the stretch and crazy surrender of alpine downhill—
Chinese culture responsible for the invention
of everything except the water screw & one other thing I can't remember—
the enslavement of horses that started the whole as she said it, mess,
meaning humans and the destruction of the earth (see Paul Shepard on this),
and the kind of drumming, chanting, dancing that makes your brain shut up,
and I miss her achingly, sun on her front step and tea,
talking about absolutely younameit, avec bibliography,
and she told me Love isn't everything,
but it turns out it also is.

I know that 3 lines later will be the linden tree.
Wind across the plaza, a shudder of petals.

You'll go on,
even in death,
the remembered weather of that day:
a glare, but buoyant somehow, so much light.

We're all there,
gathered, parting, slowly walking away, not turning,
leaving you both here and never.

A handful of Spanish soil for your thoughts, my love,
for later, when I'll need it.

Door // Wind // Door

You can't go back from what goes forward in dream
—Robert Duncan

Buddleia blossoms crumble to the touch.
It's a dream of dreaming where you speak to me.

It's your exact cadence.

We remember each other across an abyss,
a cocktail party, an ocean, a set of mountains: the Urals, the Caucasus,

soft pillows, open pages of Duino Elegies in high German,
our paper-strewn kitchen table, the Russian steppes rampant
with yellow poppies, the mowing scene in Anna K,
thick roast beef sandwiches on rye with horseradish
in a kosher dive down by Houghton.

I have said your name in seven languages, 3 of them extinct.

I know your favorite color, the fragrance of your body after a night
of love, or poems, after Coltrane's fierce unbidden soar
heard in the doorway of the Blue Note.

I rolled the car, you rolled the car.
You drove carefully, me never.

I serve you chrysanthemum tea in bed, we drink icy shots
of Aquavit on the train to Zagreb.

We never went to China or Persia.

We had white cats, we had black cats.

I wore red silk in one life. You ate thin crêpes, dosed absinthe
in endless café debate with your crowd of expatriate painters, poets.
I was unutterably famous. Your father was my lover.

We had so much to say,
we never spoke; you had my sister.

You didn't come home. We'd spend days in bed. My skin smells of you,
my hair over your chest.

I will never miss you.
I will always miss you.

Shiva dances where we are buried in each other's arms.

I go on. Marry another.

I bear the mark of your earnest child in my voice.
I plant a garden in circles of blue

timed to go off in a catapult of bloom, our own Sissinghurst.

I dial your number 20 years later. I can hear you,
your part of our conversation
a constant
long after your death, your next marriage, your blind drunk ramblings.

Here the horses graze lazy in the canyon *vegas*.
They'll till here soon.
I'll call you and tell you then.

Walking Faster than the Speed of Falling, Seeing Stars

Pearl of timed sound, round, nacreous,
distant plunge of fire:
scarlet runner open to the angle of summer's eager door
hinged awake, the furl/unfurl and curl of corn: say tassel and keep going.

Put in seed we did, and waited; breathless anticipation.

Sugar   potash   blanch of rain

New grapes encircling the spar of mullein.
Not an iota of complaint reached the garden; tempers flared but somehow
came to a serenity of abandoned lavish.

Delicata and *tomatillo*.
How my longing exceeds my capabilities to select: say yes to this *habanero*,
no to that pushy rhizome.

An intruder has chosen to dream itself in, sinking roots,
though we know the gravity of dream is flight.

I too stay,

willing to stand on line in carelessly broken ground, waiting
patiently for the canyon's generous handout: on the dole of wet,
the enthusiastic radiance of day, the Milky Way's curled vast spectacular
of cream effervescent,
Perseid parade of plummet and gasp, your name in my mouth.

Red hollyhocks are the door to the next world: I'll go, take me, I say.

The road to shower and sheen and raspberries in La Cueva soon.
In Guadalupita, friends have babies and marry;
life goes tumultuously on.

I'm glad I saw the river so I know
not to push what is already and always moving.

What adventure doesn't begin with death or marriage,
what morning does not choose wind,
what garden, storm, or at least fervent tillage.

Tell me this, when I go: will the emptiness finally arrive,
and who will tell the story of the bears?

The Angels that Break Us

...break you open out of who you are...
—Rainer Maria Rilke

Love is a controlled burn gone haywire.

If high winds prevail,
the canopy will catch and you'll be swept into flame,
wishing you had done some stretching before the full asana of surrender.

...If I were with you, the impassioned poet says,
I would put hot and cold compresses on your...

He tells me, poetically,
I want to do with you, Neruda's gorgeous line:
what spring does with the cherry trees.

Maybe I need to say something memorable back.

I want to do with you,
I should say, in my best bedtime voice,
what autumn does to the maples, so drop your leaves right now baby.
Or what winter does to the pine boughs, or what summer does to the Milky Way.

Maybe a month-by-month erotic weather watch.

Is that too abstruse?

Poetry doesn't seem needed here—instead, a train car, a cigar, a suggestive
aside, a torrent of roses, 380-stitch designer sheets, a cloud bank, a gold ring,
paella and Rioja, very dark, a clock tower; no, that's dangerous....

Lingerie, I think—do I even remember—the clover and winter rye soft lawn
and champagne in crystal too good for outside—is this how it's done?

I know what—I'll say I want to be your cupcake,
I want to be 3 sweet bites and a lap full of crumbs,
a plaything for your mouth.

I want you to peel off my skirt, pleat by pleat,
and expose me to your appetite.

I want to be so good you can't get enough and more is too much,
but you just keep going like there's no tomorrow, which there isn't;
I learned the hard way.

Stop, not that again.

Try:
You are the elk herd, new velveted antlers, seen high on the ridge
across from Joe's oat field he's planted for the second year,
and I adore its shade of verdancy like no other, and they're safe, the elk,
I mean, safe until September, but after that, watch out, permits will be issued.

Men in camouflage, looking like the woods they are not,
head out into the forest
half-cocked,
ready to take flesh and bone, sleek skin.

Throw corn meal, make the prayer; blood shall spill,
hillsides ring, split by gunfire, the enflame of hunt become feast.

Bring your hunger, bring your eager mouth, I'll say,
I'll say that this time.

Torn Sutras

Is love, rice in a jar,
no need to give back an egg?
—Amy Tan

The wild horse of the love body
is oddly willing
to be ridden by such as us.

Master and student alike may stroke the passionate belly of the tiger.
No one to blame or congratulate.

The magnificent ears of the elephant
swing wide in the true, or false, woods of the poet
whose words do often throw wisdom out windows.

We are all such forgetters, and our practice is lousy with it.

I'll meet you halfway.

Neither darkness nor illumination.
Neither dream nor dharma.

Instead, lovers
on a train to each other.

The station where both were all the time
anyway going.

Porters and steaming cups of coffee,
fields clipping past.

Bearing little luggage, crossing the great rivers of the East
named for the disappeared ones.

At dusk, of course, at journey's end,

finding each other
late, beneath jittery
streetlight,

no matter what,
and entirely because
of, what came before.

96% Proof of Disappearance

The canyon wren created the world,
the mockingbird is the patron saint of poets.

Close the fractal piece of your brain.

Ask God for the answer to terror.
Go to Thailand. Take the waves in full measure;
be yourself tsunami. Find the shape of true horizon.

You drank your way out of my heart.
Spell absence: v o d k a.
I face left and miss you in the helix of willing, our house, the one we wrote.

Fly, instead, in an armor of song.

Not even the mockingbird knows his own notes,
but he can sing frog and five colors.

Smile when you think.

Hang me out to dry, on cottonwood peeled of bark;
I'll forget nothing, not the wing's ardent lift, not the curved bell of body.

As damp to wool, is mordant to saturate:
we'll both dye, and be glad of it.

Ask permission and eschew iron.

As antler is the deer's music,
I am for you this night, as always.

Leave a garden untilled for us
in the tended acres of your poems.

Sweetness is a desire that begins

on the iris's tongue:
pistil-feathered, stamen-stuttered,
petal-striped one.

Say bloom and, saying, bloom.
Sift that sugar
into the cake of language.

If you could turn your heart into a cow stall,

you could be grateful for lambsquarters,
you would call dandelion "Friend of my liver."
You would see tonic in what is green, bitter and wholly given.

Who is this someone hearing and telling?
When risen into rose, we are that sweetness in the heart:
honey, beads of amber, pure joy
before flower and after flower.

Our rivers are rivers and rivers flow and move to the sea,
which is our dying,

which is our breath and our belief; and the ticking greenlit
nimbus of the cottonwoods which lives inside our bones
serves as breakfast, and we are called, really, by name, to table.

After the fright of dying,
the joy of having arrived

in the canyon,
where quiet settles even in the beaver's den,
his logging business stilled.
Water's music, gush and gurgle
of early spring melt is heard.

The ear participates and helps arrange marriages
between the duck
and the water's broken surface.

What if we married our silence that way?

Or the blue of the sky married the arc of the sea turtle's back?
Or wind in thick pines wed the violin's heart-splitting cry
heard on the steps of the Uffizi?
Or the widow married, finally, the view?

The door is round and open!
Don't go back to sleep!

Stay outside
where a large rhyme scheme is occurring
this very minute,
and the horizon constantly scans 4 beats to the ridgeline.

Think about this for a second,

and you'd pitch a tent by that river, eat figs
and melons, soft cheese,
and drink the wine of remembering.

Your heart would acquire the beat of the hummingbird's wings in flight.
You'd whirr and hover,
staying utterly in place,
making 1000 moans.

Go mad with love
as your face shines, fully,
you moon, you.

All night, rinse your hands in tears.

All night, rinse your hands in the dreams of silvery fish.

Wake to the call of mourning doves.

How clean the sun when seen in its own idea.
How lit the day when it flows from a night of weeping.

How lit the day when rivered by no ideas
but a current of presence singing.

How precious the marriage of wind to bough.
How steadfast the river's current running to blue and salt.

If I were a fish, I would swim

No quiero otro...no hay...hay....
—Nellie Furtado

Blue is the last layer in the earth's atmosphere,
so say chrysanthemum petals on the box of God.

In dream you pressed into me, a melting from earth to air and back.
I tasted the whir of a thousand zakuris spinning the flavor of mulberry
from silk into speech.

Why wait to plant tree peonies?
Press soil beneath your palm,
push seeds into their certain cotyledon future.

Talk me into garden after garden.

I would be vine to your trunk, tendrils blossoming, and later
will be the wine in your mouth
grapes imagine themselves towards.

This as well as cling and tangle.
We'll learn what swallows know,
cattails remember, the pond reminds.

Wisteria leaves crinkle and fall, as in the lexicon of Bosque
written in crane swoop and the history of mergansers,
on the hacienda's balcony: fiery Frida, ghost of Lorca.

I learn the words in Spanish for this love, this season;
guns, heretic passion and all.
I have and become a dictionary bilingual in joy, conjugating verbs of delight,
fluent in entwine and morning, sweet after desire.

There's sparkle in the blue jay's eyes, new to us, and turquoise
spilling up from ancient copper mines:
the medicine of eager love.

Come to my house and see for yourself.
Spoken valuable at long last,
gold of fierce saying, words come true.

Step by Step

To track a barn swallow presupposes a barn,
posits the horse, the house, the wife.

To track a swallow, look for a print of absence,
the metatarsal registering weakly,
the flight inherent in the step.

To track a swallow, you will need to first imagine rain,
then a season, a latitude, a hemisphere
and, lastly, a world.

Surely somewhere in the spin and drift of the cosmos there is mud.

Imagine this back down.
Where soil is wet is a when.
In that when, swallows may build a nest.

Count the minutes of flight,
multiply by the rare occurrence of encounter.

To track the swallow, dream of rivers.
Kneel down on all fours.
Trace the gait along the eastern bank until you find the place
where whatever was resisting the evening's darkening heart
soars off above.

In the serrated moonlight on the water's silken surface,
look closely.
Turn towards home.

Surely a swallow will find you soon.

Textile of Rain

There was a cloudburst in my morning
68° Fahrenheit and rising.

I was velvet, vetiver, and echo;
the perfume was dream and dogwood.
Sometimes magnolia, anyway, Southern and East.

Had I a crisis involving passion, the painted elephants of Sri Lanka,
cardinals, or a 4-wheel-drive pickup
in a certain shade of teal,
I would certainly let you know.

You might shiver to find me so beloved,
so out and out moonlight, Grenada and olives.

Wheat and grapes would seesaw through my attention;
riffled skin of creek and density of Brahms
become my weather and new lover both.

Don't look for me here.

I am the silence between these lines:
prayers spun on a silk reel,
drizzle through canopy of maple's turning.

Gold coined by sycamore and birch
is the wealth of the Ancient Ones who walked here.
They live in the names of moving water,
clear streams' secret ramble.

Thoroughly Lyric

If color spoke yellow, we'd say buzz of honey is this:
mercurial appearance, 4-petaled,
puckered lips for kiss of whirr; we'd be insect, be flutter and sip.

Any caress of wind lifts my heart entire these days.

Today the scones taught color theory,
& cry of red-winged blackbirds pierces me sweet.

Black ants, their bodies a secret of gold burnish,
invent armor.

The landscape re-coalesces
into holy matrimony: the pattern of matter.

Grains of fragrant loam
make a languor of real.
Take it as read.

Roll onto your side; dream deep.
Make the love that grows a house finch,
a carbon molecule, a sunflower, a pine cone.

Watch the accordion unfolding of the utterly phenomenal
into rose bush and usnea lichen.

Mold is so astonishing!

The ponderosa pine, on the whole: impossibly marvelous.

The sing that starts inside
weds me faithful to feather and stamen.

I'm imperturbably floral and conversant in pond and Steller's jay.
Well-versed in hawthorn, blossom and bud,
bilingual by way of sandstone and frog song.

Stand unequivocally in awe
of dispersed dandelion, crescendo of raven, dash of nuthatch,
smidgen of wild mustard.

No bones about it,
this warmth on my skin is delicious and irrevocable.

I wear the ring of the world, am bride to the season, *fiancée* of blue blue sky.
Prima nocta, every night,
I'm always virgin, ever a beginner; astounded and practiced:
take me as bedrock.

We'll be seduced by epiphany of deciduous,
wooed and wowed to slow,
court at the incremental speed of tendril, papery wasp nest.

Swallows overhead remind me of certain flavors
hush-hush inside the bedchambers of the constantly ardent.

The hummingbird's fierce morsel of a heart races,
even while asleep.

What does this make you think of right now, this very minute?

I want to invent an embrace
good enough to mirror this day's glamour.

Come up with the Kama Sutra of spring,
a manual for the sensually vernal.
Go twin; double my capacity for swoon and surrender.

Admiration is for tourists.
I want a permanent address in this loving.

Not to mention Persian lilies,
columbines and near-black irises
a mere 2 gardens away;
but, like Zeno's arrow, I can't get there.

My now and here is so huge,
I am windchime, flicker's metal rat-a-tat, riveted.
The far and close of canyon
magnets us to this instant.

We grow intimate iron,
strong enough to wax and wane,
rush straight still,
shine in place.

The Uncertainty Principle of

looking, my love, may I find you always in sounds of water; when far,
your nearness, the inverse square of longing:
the equilateral sides of a trapezoid, entanglement of charmed particles, you rise

and fall, as linen on the breath of the newly dead.
Your heart beats in thin threads of *ito-ochi*,
strands that connect the malachite rush of secret cataract, the mysterious one

known only to the blue-eyed herds of Pemako.
I made promises of iron, wore out shoes and a staff,
seeking you through meadow, bog, on cliff edge,

harsh moraine and turbulent snow melt;
lost my balance, knock-kneed to the fault line,
traveled to the knotted interiors of ancient stories, traversed day for night,

came out once upon a time, forever after,
a pirate, a parrot, a princess, a stork; hedgehog, clock stockings.
I became and became, as what rose and dropped back into cloud

fell again into the colorless green of idea.
I believed in wave and rapid, swore allegiance to current, clung to rush and rock,
gave myself finally, utterly, to spume and thundering smoke.

Cross my palm with river and I'll tell you the downstream version,
the pitch and yaw of this fine craft, ours.
Yar, my darling, very,

& running in esplanades of thirst and quench, drought and drench.
As ravines deep in the mountain's secret heart tumble in tangle of ferns and
undergrowth, blue poppies, rhododendron, pagoda lilies, whorl after whorl,

coppery primula, tilt into encompassed scree-bound plummet, bedrock
of sudden love, splash of rejoice, springs given to rivulet, sluice and prance.
I'll race you towards our life.

Let's keep it to a murmur, pass wet between us as tea between long-time lovers.
Nothing loves the floodplain as much as the small ones that hop and scratch
in sand; we could be alluvial as they, curious excess,

a celebration of sweet waters and froth, the minted summer afternoon
into dusk, the Rufous hummingbirds' coupled sojourn
over long expanse of seas heading always home.

Woven So Entire

I'll never fall out of this loving;
from where to where could I fall?

When held in canyon, by riverbank,
in blaze of starfire or inky pitch of night,

what could I be but desert varnish wept onto rockface?
Turned by wind into purely music, desire's fabric,

homespun for the Beloved, girdle for his waist.
O most beautiful one,

I have nothing to say anymore.
Love has woven me a coat of quiet.

Acknowledgments

"There's No Place the White Clouds Can't Go" appeared in *Sacred Fire Magazine*, Issue 5.

Cover art from "The Tree of Life" by Gustav Klimt (PD-1923); photo of the author by Steve Collector; cover and interior book design by Diane Kistner (dkistner@futurecycle.org); Chaparral Pro text with Bispo titling

About FutureCycle Press

FutureCycle Press is dedicated to publishing lasting English-language poetry and flash fiction books, chapbooks, and anthologies in both print-on-demand and ebook formats. Founded in 2007 by long-time independent editor/publishers and partners Diane Kistner and Robert S. King, the press incorporated as a nonprofit in 2012. A number of our editors are distinguished poets and authors in their own right, and we have been actively involved in the small press movement going back to the early seventies.

The FutureCycle Poetry Book Prize and honorarium is awarded annually for the best full-length volume of poetry we publish in a calendar year. Introduced in 2013, our Good Works projects are devoted to issues of global significance, with all proceeds donated to a related worthy cause. We are dedicated to giving all authors we publish the care their work deserves, making our catalog of titles the most distinguished it can be, and paying forward any earnings to fund more great books.

We've learned a few things about independent publishing over the years. We've also evolved a unique, resilient publishing model that allows us to focus mainly on vetting and preserving for posterity the most books of exceptional quality without becoming overwhelmed with bookkeeping and mailing, fund-raising activities, or taxing editorial and production "bubbles." To find out more about what we are doing, come see us at www.futurecycle.org.

The FutureCycle Poetry Book Prize

All full-length volumes of poetry published by FutureCycle Press in a given calendar year are considered for the annual FutureCycle Poetry Book Prize. This allows us to consider each submission on its own merits, outside of the context of a contest. Too, the judges see the finished book, which will have benefitted from the beautiful book design and strong editorial gloss we are famous for.

The book ranked the best in judging is announced as the prize-winner in the subsequent year. There is no fixed monetary award; instead, the winning poet receives an honorarium of 20% of the total net royalties from all poetry books and chapbooks the press sold online in the year the winning book was published. The winner is also accorded the honor of judging the next year's competition.